50 Delicious Holiday Baking Recipes

By: Kelly Johnson

Table of Contents

- Classic Gingerbread Cookies
- Sugar Cookie Cutouts
- Chocolate Peppermint Bark
- Eggnog Pound Cake
- Cranberry Orange Scones
- Cinnamon Rolls with Cream Cheese Icing
- Pecan Pie Bars
- Shortbread Cookies
- Snickerdoodle Cookies
- Spiced Apple Cake
- Pumpkin Pie
- Red Velvet Cupcakes
- Almond Crescents
- Chocolate Chip Cranberry Cookies
- Yule Log Cake
- Mint Chocolate Brownies
- Poppy Seed Rolls
- Fruitcake Cookies
- Mocha Fudge
- Chocolate-Dipped Pretzels
- Cherry Almond Biscotti
- Caramel Pecan Bars
- Walnut Fudge
- Snowball Cookies
- Eggnog Cheesecake
- Apple Cinnamon Streusel Muffins
- Maple Pecan Tarts
- Holiday Spice Cake
- Rum Balls
- Hazelnut Chocolate Truffles
- Chocolate Mint Cupcakes
- Carrot Cake with Cream Cheese Frosting
- Holiday Rugelach
- Toffee Pecan Cookies
- Cranberry Walnut Bread

- Chocolate Truffle Cookies
- Apple Pie Bars
- Pumpkin Chocolate Chip Muffins
- Lemon Poppy Seed Cake
- Double Chocolate Peppermint Cookies
- Raspberry Almond Thumbprint Cookies
- Sticky Buns with Caramel Sauce
- Sweet Potato Pie
- Chocolate Crinkle Cookies
- Lemon Snowflakes
- Orange Cranberry Loaf Cake
- Maple Walnut Fudge
- Pecan Praline Cookies
- Cherry Chocolate Chunk Cookies
- Hazelnut Linzer Cookies

Classic Gingerbread Cookies

Ingredients:

- 3 1/4 cups all-purpose flour
- 1 1/2 teaspoons baking soda
- 1 tablespoon ground ginger
- 1 tablespoon ground cinnamon
- 1/2 teaspoon ground cloves
- 1/2 teaspoon ground nutmeg
- 1/2 teaspoon salt
- 3/4 cup unsalted butter, softened
- 1/2 cup dark brown sugar, packed
- 1 large egg
- 1/2 cup unsulfured molasses
- 1 tablespoon fresh grated ginger (optional, for added depth)
- 1 teaspoon vanilla extract

For decorating (optional):

- Royal icing or powdered sugar glaze
- Sprinkles, colored sugar, or candy for decoration

Instructions:

1. **Prepare dry ingredients:**
   In a large bowl, whisk together the flour, baking soda, ground ginger, cinnamon, cloves, nutmeg, and salt. Set aside.
2. **Cream butter and sugar:**
   In another large bowl, beat the softened butter and brown sugar with an electric mixer until light and fluffy, about 2-3 minutes.
3. **Add wet ingredients:**
   Add the egg, molasses, and vanilla extract (and fresh ginger, if using) to the butter mixture, and beat until combined.
4. **Combine wet and dry ingredients:**
   Gradually add the dry flour mixture to the wet ingredients, mixing on low speed until just combined. The dough will be thick and slightly sticky.
5. **Chill the dough:**
   Divide the dough into two portions, wrap each in plastic wrap, and refrigerate for at least 2 hours or overnight. Chilling helps the dough firm up and makes rolling easier.

6. **Preheat the oven:**
   Preheat the oven to 350°F (175°C). Line two baking sheets with parchment paper.
7. **Roll out the dough:**
   On a lightly floured surface, roll out one portion of dough to about 1/8 inch thickness. Use cookie cutters to cut out shapes (such as gingerbread men, stars, or hearts). Place the cookies on the prepared baking sheets, spacing them about 1 inch apart.
8. **Bake the cookies:**
   Bake the cookies for 8-10 minutes, or until the edges are firm and the centers are slightly soft. The cookies will continue to firm up as they cool.
9. **Cool and decorate:**
   Allow the cookies to cool on the baking sheets for 5 minutes before transferring them to wire racks to cool completely. Once cooled, decorate with royal icing, sprinkles, or a simple powdered sugar glaze.

Sugar Cookie Cutouts

Ingredients:

- 3 cups all-purpose flour
- 3/4 teaspoon baking powder
- 1/4 teaspoon salt
- 1 cup unsalted butter, softened
- 1 cup granulated sugar
- 1 large egg
- 1 teaspoon vanilla extract
- 1/4 teaspoon almond extract (optional)

Instructions:

1. **Mix dry ingredients:** In a bowl, whisk together flour, baking powder, and salt. Set aside.
2. **Cream butter and sugar:** Beat the butter and sugar until light and fluffy. Add the egg, vanilla, and almond extract, mixing until combined.
3. **Combine:** Gradually add the dry ingredients, mixing just until the dough forms.
4. **Chill:** Divide dough in half, flatten into disks, wrap in plastic, and chill for 1 hour.
5. **Roll and cut:** Roll out on a floured surface to 1/4 inch thickness. Use cookie cutters for shapes.
6. **Bake:** Place cutouts on parchment-lined baking sheets and bake at 350°F (175°C) for 8-10 minutes, until edges are lightly golden.
7. **Cool and decorate:** Let cool completely before decorating with icing or sprinkles.

Chocolate Peppermint Bark

Ingredients:

- 12 ounces dark chocolate, chopped
- 12 ounces white chocolate, chopped
- 1/2 teaspoon peppermint extract
- 1/2 cup crushed candy canes

Instructions:

1. **Prepare pan:** Line a baking sheet with parchment paper.
2. **Melt dark chocolate:** Melt in a heatproof bowl over a simmering pot of water (double boiler) or in the microwave in 20-second intervals. Spread evenly onto the lined sheet. Chill for 15 minutes.
3. **Melt white chocolate:** Repeat the process with the white chocolate, then stir in peppermint extract. Spread over the hardened dark chocolate layer.
4. **Add candy canes:** Sprinkle crushed candy canes over the top, pressing them lightly to adhere.
5. **Chill:** Refrigerate for 1 hour, or until completely set.
6. **Break into pieces:** Use your hands or a knife to break the bark into chunks.

Eggnog Pound Cake

Ingredients:

- 2 1/4 cups all-purpose flour
- 1 teaspoon baking powder
- 1/2 teaspoon salt
- 1/2 teaspoon ground nutmeg
- 1 cup unsalted butter, softened
- 2 cups granulated sugar
- 4 large eggs
- 1 teaspoon vanilla extract
- 1 teaspoon rum extract (optional)
- 1 cup eggnog

Instructions:

1. **Prepare oven and pan:** Preheat oven to 350°F (175°C). Grease and flour a bundt or loaf pan.
2. **Mix dry ingredients:** In a bowl, whisk together flour, baking powder, salt, and nutmeg.
3. **Cream butter and sugar:** Beat butter and sugar until fluffy. Add eggs one at a time, mixing well. Stir in vanilla and rum extract.
4. **Alternate additions:** Gradually add dry ingredients and eggnog, alternating between the two, starting and ending with the flour mixture.
5. **Bake:** Pour batter into the prepared pan and bake for 55-65 minutes, or until a toothpick inserted into the center comes out clean.
6. **Cool:** Let the cake cool in the pan for 10 minutes before transferring to a wire rack.
7. **Optional glaze:** Drizzle with a simple glaze made from powdered sugar and a splash of eggnog.

Cranberry Orange Scones

Ingredients:

- 2 cups all-purpose flour
- 1/4 cup granulated sugar
- 1 tablespoon baking powder
- 1/2 teaspoon salt
- 1/2 cup cold unsalted butter, cubed
- 1/2 cup dried cranberries
- Zest of 1 orange
- 2/3 cup heavy cream
- 1 large egg

Instructions:

1. **Mix dry ingredients:** Combine flour, sugar, baking powder, and salt in a bowl.
2. **Cut in butter:** Add butter and mix until the texture is crumbly.
3. **Add flavorings:** Stir in cranberries and orange zest.
4. **Combine wet ingredients:** Whisk cream and egg, then add to the dry mixture until just combined.
5. **Shape and bake:** Pat dough into a circle, cut into wedges, and bake at 400°F (200°C) for 15-18 minutes.

Cinnamon Rolls with Cream Cheese Icing

Ingredients:

Dough:

- 3 1/4 cups all-purpose flour
- 1/4 cup granulated sugar
- 2 1/4 teaspoons instant yeast
- 1/2 teaspoon salt
- 1/2 cup whole milk
- 1/4 cup unsalted butter, melted
- 2 large eggs

Filling:

- 1/2 cup brown sugar
- 2 tablespoons ground cinnamon
- 1/4 cup unsalted butter, softened

Icing:

- 4 ounces cream cheese, softened
- 1/4 cup unsalted butter, softened
- 1 cup powdered sugar
- 1 teaspoon vanilla extract

Instructions:

1. **Prepare dough:** Mix dry ingredients, add wet ingredients, knead, and let rise until doubled.
2. **Add filling:** Roll dough into a rectangle, spread with butter, sprinkle cinnamon sugar, then roll and slice.
3. **Bake:** Place rolls in a greased pan, let rise, then bake at 350°F (175°C) for 25-30 minutes.
4. **Icing:** Beat cream cheese, butter, sugar, and vanilla, then spread on warm rolls.

Pecan Pie Bars

Ingredients:

- 2 cups all-purpose flour
- 1/2 cup powdered sugar
- 1 cup cold unsalted butter
- 3 large eggs
- 1 cup corn syrup
- 1 cup granulated sugar
- 2 tablespoons unsalted butter, melted
- 1 teaspoon vanilla extract
- 1 1/2 cups chopped pecans

Instructions:

1. **Make crust:** Combine flour, powdered sugar, and butter, then press into a baking pan. Bake at 350°F (175°C) for 20 minutes.
2. **Prepare filling:** Whisk eggs, corn syrup, sugar, melted butter, and vanilla. Stir in pecans.
3. **Bake:** Pour filling over crust and bake for 25-30 minutes. Cool before slicing.

Shortbread Cookies

Ingredients:

- 2 cups all-purpose flour
- 1/2 cup powdered sugar
- 1 cup unsalted butter, softened
- 1 teaspoon vanilla extract

Instructions:

1. **Mix dough:** Combine flour, sugar, butter, and vanilla until crumbly, then form into a dough.
2. **Shape and bake:** Roll out dough, cut into shapes, and bake at 350°F (175°C) for 12-15 minutes.

Snickerdoodle Cookies

Ingredients:

- 2 3/4 cups all-purpose flour
- 1/2 teaspoon salt
- 2 teaspoons cream of tartar
- 1 teaspoon baking soda
- 1 cup unsalted butter, softened
- 1 1/2 cups granulated sugar
- 2 large eggs
- 3 tablespoons granulated sugar
- 1 tablespoon ground cinnamon

Instructions:

1. **Make dough:** Cream butter and sugar, add eggs, then mix in dry ingredients.
2. **Coat:** Shape dough into balls and roll in cinnamon-sugar mixture.
3. **Bake:** Bake at 375°F (190°C) for 8-10 minutes.

Spiced Apple Cake

Ingredients:

- 2 cups all-purpose flour
- 1 1/2 teaspoons baking powder
- 1/2 teaspoon baking soda
- 1 teaspoon ground cinnamon
- 1/2 teaspoon ground nutmeg
- 1/2 teaspoon ground cloves
- 1/4 teaspoon salt
- 1/2 cup unsalted butter, softened
- 1 cup granulated sugar
- 2 large eggs
- 1/2 cup applesauce
- 2 cups peeled, chopped apples

Instructions:

1. **Mix batter:** Cream butter and sugar, add eggs, then stir in dry ingredients alternately with applesauce. Fold in apples.
2. **Bake:** Pour batter into a greased pan and bake at 350°F (175°C) for 45-50 minutes.

Pumpkin Pie

Ingredients:

- 1 9-inch pie crust
- 3/4 cup granulated sugar
- 1 teaspoon ground cinnamon
- 1/2 teaspoon ground ginger
- 1/4 teaspoon ground cloves
- 1/2 teaspoon salt
- 2 large eggs
- 1 (15-ounce) can pumpkin puree
- 1 (12-ounce) can evaporated milk

Instructions:

1. **Prepare filling:** Mix sugar, spices, salt, eggs, pumpkin, and milk until smooth.
2. **Assemble pie:** Pour filling into crust.
3. **Bake:** Bake at 425°F (220°C) for 15 minutes, then lower temperature to 350°F (175°C) and bake for 40-50 minutes.

Red Velvet Cupcakes

Ingredients:

- 2 1/2 cups all-purpose flour
- 1/4 cup cocoa powder
- 1 teaspoon baking soda
- 1/2 teaspoon salt
- 1/2 cup unsalted butter, softened
- 1 1/2 cups granulated sugar
- 2 large eggs
- 1 cup buttermilk
- 2 tablespoons red food coloring
- 1 teaspoon vanilla extract
- 1 teaspoon white vinegar

Instructions:

1. **Make batter:** Mix dry ingredients. Cream butter and sugar, add eggs, and mix in buttermilk, food coloring, vanilla, and vinegar. Combine wet and dry ingredients.
2. **Bake:** Pour into cupcake liners and bake at 350°F (175°C) for 20-22 minutes.

Almond Crescents

Ingredients:

- 1 cup unsalted butter, softened
- 2/3 cup powdered sugar
- 1 teaspoon vanilla extract
- 1/2 teaspoon almond extract
- 2 cups all-purpose flour
- 1 cup finely chopped almonds

Instructions:

1. **Mix dough:** Cream butter, sugar, and extracts. Add flour and almonds, mixing until combined.
2. **Shape and bake:** Form dough into crescent shapes and bake at 350°F (175°C) for 15-20 minutes.
3. **Coat:** While warm, roll in powdered sugar.

Chocolate Chip Cranberry Cookies

Ingredients:

- 2 1/4 cups all-purpose flour
- 1/2 teaspoon baking soda
- 1/2 teaspoon salt
- 1 cup unsalted butter, softened
- 3/4 cup granulated sugar
- 3/4 cup brown sugar
- 1 teaspoon vanilla extract
- 2 large eggs
- 1 cup dried cranberries
- 1 cup semi-sweet chocolate chips

Instructions:

1. **Mix dry ingredients:** Combine flour, baking soda, and salt in a bowl.
2. **Cream butter and sugars:** Beat butter, granulated sugar, and brown sugar until fluffy. Add vanilla and eggs one at a time.
3. **Combine:** Gradually mix in dry ingredients, then fold in cranberries and chocolate chips.
4. **Bake:** Drop spoonfuls of dough onto a baking sheet and bake at 350°F (175°C) for 10-12 minutes.

Yule Log Cake

Ingredients:

Cake:

- 3/4 cup all-purpose flour
- 1/3 cup cocoa powder
- 1 teaspoon baking powder
- 1/4 teaspoon salt
- 4 large eggs
- 3/4 cup granulated sugar
- 1 teaspoon vanilla extract

Filling:

- 1 cup heavy cream
- 2 tablespoons powdered sugar
- 1 teaspoon vanilla extract

Frosting:

- 1 1/2 cups chocolate ganache or buttercream

Instructions:

1. **Make cake:** Whisk dry ingredients. Beat eggs and sugar until thick, then fold in dry mix. Spread batter in a jelly roll pan and bake at 375°F (190°C) for 10 minutes.
2. **Roll and cool:** Turn cake onto a towel, roll, and cool.
3. **Fill and frost:** Unroll, add whipped cream filling, re-roll, and frost with ganache.

Mint Chocolate Brownies

Ingredients:

- 1/2 cup unsalted butter, melted
- 1 cup granulated sugar
- 2 large eggs
- 1 teaspoon vanilla extract
- 1/3 cup cocoa powder
- 1/2 cup all-purpose flour
- 1/4 teaspoon salt
- 1/4 teaspoon baking powder
- 1/2 teaspoon peppermint extract

Instructions:

1. **Prepare batter:** Combine butter, sugar, eggs, vanilla, and peppermint extract. Stir in cocoa, flour, salt, and baking powder.
2. **Bake:** Spread batter in a greased pan and bake at 350°F (175°C) for 20-25 minutes.
3. **Optional glaze:** Top with chocolate ganache and crushed peppermint candies.

Poppy Seed Rolls

Ingredients:

- 2 1/2 cups all-purpose flour
- 1/2 cup granulated sugar
- 1/4 teaspoon salt
- 1/2 cup milk, warmed
- 1 packet active dry yeast
- 1/4 cup unsalted butter, melted
- 2 large eggs
- 3/4 cup poppy seed filling (store-bought or homemade)

Instructions:

1. **Make dough:** Dissolve yeast in warm milk. Mix flour, sugar, and salt. Add yeast mixture, butter, and eggs. Knead until smooth. Let rise until doubled.
2. **Fill and roll:** Roll dough into a rectangle, spread with poppy seed filling, then roll tightly.
3. **Bake:** Place on a baking sheet, let rise, and bake at 350°F (175°C) for 25-30 minutes.

Fruitcake Cookies

Ingredients:

- 1 cup unsalted butter, softened
- 1 cup brown sugar
- 2 large eggs
- 1 teaspoon vanilla extract
- 2 cups all-purpose flour
- 1/2 teaspoon baking powder
- 1/2 teaspoon salt
- 1/2 teaspoon cinnamon
- 1/2 cup candied cherries, chopped
- 1/2 cup candied pineapple, chopped
- 1/2 cup chopped pecans

Instructions:

1. **Mix dough:** Cream butter and sugar. Add eggs and vanilla, then mix in dry ingredients. Fold in candied fruits and nuts.
2. **Bake:** Drop dough onto baking sheets and bake at 350°F (175°C) for 12-15 minutes.

Mocha Fudge

Ingredients:

- 3 cups semi-sweet chocolate chips
- 1 (14-ounce) can sweetened condensed milk
- 2 tablespoons instant coffee granules
- 1 teaspoon vanilla extract

Instructions:

1. **Melt and mix:** In a saucepan, melt chocolate chips and condensed milk over low heat. Stir in coffee granules and vanilla.
2. **Set fudge:** Pour into a lined pan, smooth the top, and refrigerate until firm.
3. **Cut:** Slice into squares before serving.

Chocolate-Dipped Pretzels

Ingredients:

- 12 ounces semi-sweet chocolate, melted
- 1 bag pretzel rods or twists
- 1/4 cup sprinkles or crushed nuts

Instructions:

1. **Dip pretzels:** Dip each pretzel into melted chocolate, allowing excess to drip off.
2. **Decorate:** Sprinkle with toppings while the chocolate is wet.
3. **Set:** Place on parchment paper and let chocolate harden.

Cherry Almond Biscotti

Ingredients:

- 2 1/4 cups all-purpose flour
- 1 teaspoon baking powder
- 1/2 teaspoon salt
- 1/2 cup unsalted butter, softened
- 3/4 cup granulated sugar
- 2 large eggs
- 1 teaspoon almond extract
- 1/2 cup dried cherries
- 1/2 cup sliced almonds

Instructions:

1. **Mix dough:** Cream butter and sugar, add eggs and almond extract, then mix in dry ingredients. Fold in cherries and almonds.
2. **Shape and bake:** Form dough into a log, bake at 350°F (175°C) for 25 minutes. Cool, slice, and bake slices for 10 minutes per side.

Caramel Pecan Bars

Ingredients:

- 2 cups all-purpose flour
- 1/2 cup powdered sugar
- 1 cup unsalted butter, softened
- 1 cup brown sugar
- 1/2 cup corn syrup
- 1/4 cup unsalted butter
- 2 cups chopped pecans

Instructions:

1. **Make crust:** Mix flour, powdered sugar, and butter, press into a pan, and bake at 350°F (175°C) for 15 minutes.
2. **Prepare topping:** Heat brown sugar, corn syrup, and butter until smooth. Stir in pecans.
3. **Bake:** Pour topping over crust and bake for 20-25 minutes. Cool before cutting into bars.

Walnut Fudge

Ingredients:

- 3 cups semi-sweet chocolate chips
- 1 (14-ounce) can sweetened condensed milk
- 1 teaspoon vanilla extract
- 1 cup chopped walnuts

Instructions:

1. **Melt and mix:** In a saucepan over low heat, melt chocolate chips and condensed milk. Remove from heat and stir in vanilla and walnuts.
2. **Set fudge:** Pour into a lined 8-inch pan, smooth the top, and refrigerate until firm.
3. **Cut:** Slice into squares before serving.

Snowball Cookies

Ingredients:

- 1 cup unsalted butter, softened
- 1/2 cup powdered sugar, plus extra for coating
- 1 teaspoon vanilla extract
- 2 1/4 cups all-purpose flour
- 1/4 teaspoon salt
- 1 cup finely chopped pecans or walnuts

Instructions:

1. **Make dough:** Cream butter and powdered sugar. Mix in vanilla, then stir in flour, salt, and nuts.
2. **Bake:** Roll dough into balls and place on a baking sheet. Bake at 350°F (175°C) for 12-15 minutes.
3. **Coat:** Roll warm cookies in powdered sugar, then repeat once cooled.

Eggnog Cheesecake

Ingredients:

Crust:

- 1 1/2 cups graham cracker crumbs
- 1/4 cup granulated sugar
- 1/3 cup melted butter

Filling:

- 3 (8-ounce) packages cream cheese, softened
- 1 cup granulated sugar
- 3/4 cup eggnog
- 3 large eggs
- 2 tablespoons all-purpose flour
- 1/2 teaspoon nutmeg

Instructions:

1. **Prepare crust:** Combine crumbs, sugar, and butter, pressing into the bottom of a springform pan.
2. **Make filling:** Beat cream cheese and sugar until smooth. Add eggnog, eggs, flour, and nutmeg. Pour over crust.
3. **Bake:** Bake at 325°F (163°C) for 50-60 minutes. Cool and refrigerate before serving.

Apple Cinnamon Streusel Muffins

Ingredients:

Muffins:

- 2 cups all-purpose flour
- 2 teaspoons baking powder
- 1/2 teaspoon salt
- 1 teaspoon cinnamon
- 1/2 cup granulated sugar
- 1/2 cup brown sugar
- 2 large eggs
- 1/2 cup vegetable oil
- 1/2 cup milk
- 1 cup diced apples

Streusel:

- 1/4 cup flour
- 1/4 cup brown sugar
- 1/4 teaspoon cinnamon
- 2 tablespoons cold butter

Instructions:

1. **Mix batter:** Combine dry and wet ingredients separately, then mix together. Fold in apples.
2. **Make streusel:** Mix streusel ingredients until crumbly.
3. **Bake:** Divide batter into muffin cups, top with streusel, and bake at 375°F (190°C) for 18-22 minutes.

Maple Pecan Tarts

Ingredients:

- 1 package (9-inch) pie crust, cut into small rounds
- 1/2 cup brown sugar
- 1/3 cup maple syrup
- 2 tablespoons unsalted butter, melted
- 1 large egg
- 1/2 teaspoon vanilla extract
- 1 cup chopped pecans

Instructions:

1. **Prepare shells:** Fit pie crust rounds into mini muffin tins.
2. **Make filling:** Mix brown sugar, maple syrup, butter, egg, and vanilla. Stir in pecans.
3. **Bake:** Spoon filling into crusts and bake at 350°F (175°C) for 20-25 minutes.

Holiday Spice Cake

Ingredients:

- 2 1/2 cups all-purpose flour
- 2 teaspoons baking powder
- 1/2 teaspoon baking soda
- 1/2 teaspoon salt
- 1 teaspoon cinnamon
- 1/2 teaspoon nutmeg
- 1/4 teaspoon cloves
- 1/2 cup unsalted butter, softened
- 1 cup brown sugar
- 3 large eggs
- 1 teaspoon vanilla extract
- 1 cup buttermilk

Instructions:

1. **Mix batter:** Combine dry ingredients. Cream butter and sugar, add eggs and vanilla, then alternate mixing in dry ingredients and buttermilk.
2. **Bake:** Pour batter into a greased 9-inch pan and bake at 350°F (175°C) for 35-40 minutes.

Rum Balls

Ingredients:

- 2 cups crushed vanilla wafers
- 1 cup powdered sugar
- 1/4 cup cocoa powder
- 1 cup finely chopped pecans
- 1/3 cup dark rum
- 2 tablespoons corn syrup

Instructions:

1. **Mix ingredients:** Combine all ingredients in a large bowl.
2. **Shape:** Roll mixture into 1-inch balls.
3. **Chill:** Refrigerate until firm.

Hazelnut Chocolate Truffles

Ingredients:

- 8 ounces semi-sweet chocolate, chopped
- 1/2 cup heavy cream
- 1 teaspoon vanilla extract
- 1/2 cup ground hazelnuts

Instructions:

1. **Make ganache:** Heat cream and pour over chocolate, stirring until smooth. Add vanilla. Chill until firm.
2. **Shape:** Roll into balls and coat with ground hazelnuts.

Chocolate Mint Cupcakes

Ingredients:

Cupcakes:

- 1 cup all-purpose flour
- 1/3 cup cocoa powder
- 1/2 teaspoon baking soda
- 1/4 teaspoon salt
- 1/2 cup sugar
- 1/2 cup brown sugar
- 1/2 cup vegetable oil
- 2 large eggs
- 1/2 teaspoon peppermint extract

Frosting:

- 1 cup butter, softened
- 3 cups powdered sugar
- 1/2 teaspoon peppermint extract
- Green food coloring (optional)

Instructions:

1. **Make batter:** Combine dry and wet ingredients separately, then mix together. Fill cupcake liners and bake at 350°F (175°C) for 18-20 minutes.
2. **Frost:** Beat frosting ingredients and pipe onto cooled cupcakes.

Carrot Cake with Cream Cheese Frosting

Ingredients:

Cake:

- 2 cups all-purpose flour
- 2 teaspoons baking powder
- 1/2 teaspoon baking soda
- 1/2 teaspoon salt
- 1 teaspoon cinnamon
- 1/4 teaspoon nutmeg
- 1/4 teaspoon cloves
- 1 cup granulated sugar
- 1 cup brown sugar
- 1 cup vegetable oil
- 3 large eggs
- 2 cups grated carrots

Frosting:

- 8 ounces cream cheese, softened
- 1/4 cup unsalted butter, softened
- 2 cups powdered sugar
- 1 teaspoon vanilla extract

Instructions:

1. **Make batter:** Mix dry ingredients. Beat sugars, oil, and eggs, then fold in carrots and dry mix. Pour into pans.
2. **Bake:** Bake at 350°F (175°C) for 25-30 minutes. Cool completely.
3. **Frost:** Beat frosting ingredients and spread over cake.

Holiday Rugelach

Ingredients:

Dough:

- 2 cups all-purpose flour
- 1/4 teaspoon salt
- 1 cup unsalted butter, softened
- 8 ounces cream cheese, softened

Filling:

- 1/4 cup granulated sugar
- 1/4 cup brown sugar
- 1 teaspoon cinnamon
- 1/2 cup finely chopped walnuts
- 1/2 cup raisins
- 1/2 cup apricot or raspberry jam

Instructions:

1. **Prepare dough:** Mix flour and salt. Beat butter and cream cheese until smooth, then add flour mixture. Divide dough into 4 disks, wrap, and refrigerate for 1 hour.
2. **Add filling:** Roll dough into a circle, spread with jam, and sprinkle with a mix of sugar, cinnamon, nuts, and raisins.
3. **Shape and bake:** Cut into wedges, roll from wide to narrow end, and place on a baking sheet. Bake at 350°F (175°C) for 20-25 minutes.

Toffee Pecan Cookies

Ingredients:

- 1 cup unsalted butter, softened
- 1 cup brown sugar
- 1/2 cup granulated sugar
- 2 large eggs
- 1 teaspoon vanilla extract
- 2 1/4 cups all-purpose flour
- 1/2 teaspoon baking soda
- 1/2 teaspoon salt
- 1 cup toffee bits
- 1 cup chopped pecans

Instructions:

1. **Mix dough:** Cream butter and sugars. Beat in eggs and vanilla. Add dry ingredients, then fold in toffee bits and pecans.
2. **Bake:** Drop spoonfuls of dough onto a baking sheet and bake at 350°F (175°C) for 10-12 minutes.

Cranberry Walnut Bread

Ingredients:

- 2 cups all-purpose flour
- 1 cup granulated sugar
- 1 1/2 teaspoons baking powder
- 1/2 teaspoon salt
- 1/4 teaspoon baking soda
- 3/4 cup orange juice
- 1/4 cup melted butter
- 1 large egg
- 1 cup fresh or dried cranberries
- 1/2 cup chopped walnuts

Instructions:

1. **Mix batter:** Combine dry ingredients. Mix orange juice, butter, and egg separately, then add to dry mix. Fold in cranberries and walnuts.
2. **Bake:** Pour into a greased loaf pan and bake at 350°F (175°C) for 50-60 minutes.

Chocolate Truffle Cookies

Ingredients:

- 8 ounces semi-sweet chocolate, melted
- 1/2 cup unsalted butter, softened
- 1 cup granulated sugar
- 2 large eggs
- 1 teaspoon vanilla extract
- 1 1/2 cups all-purpose flour
- 1/4 cup cocoa powder
- 1 teaspoon baking powder
- 1/4 teaspoon salt
- Powdered sugar (for coating)

Instructions:

1. **Make dough:** Beat butter and sugar, then mix in eggs, vanilla, and melted chocolate. Add dry ingredients. Chill dough for 1 hour.
2. **Bake:** Roll dough into balls, coat with powdered sugar, and bake at 350°F (175°C) for 10-12 minutes.

Apple Pie Bars

Ingredients:

Crust:

- 2 cups all-purpose flour
- 1/2 cup granulated sugar
- 1/2 teaspoon salt
- 1 cup unsalted butter, softened

Filling:

- 5 cups peeled and sliced apples
- 1/2 cup granulated sugar
- 1 teaspoon cinnamon
- 1/4 teaspoon nutmeg

Topping:

- 1/2 cup brown sugar
- 1/2 cup flour
- 1/4 cup unsalted butter, softened

Instructions:

1. **Make crust:** Mix crust ingredients, press into a baking dish, and bake at 350°F (175°C) for 15 minutes.
2. **Add filling:** Toss apples with sugar and spices, layer over crust.
3. **Add topping and bake:** Mix topping ingredients, sprinkle over apples, and bake for 30-35 minutes.

Pumpkin Chocolate Chip Muffins

Ingredients:

- 1 3/4 cups all-purpose flour
- 1 teaspoon baking powder
- 1/2 teaspoon baking soda
- 1/2 teaspoon salt
- 1 teaspoon cinnamon
- 1/4 teaspoon nutmeg
- 3/4 cup granulated sugar
- 1/2 cup brown sugar
- 1/2 cup vegetable oil
- 2 large eggs
- 1 cup canned pumpkin
- 1/2 cup chocolate chips

Instructions:

1. **Mix batter:** Combine dry ingredients. Beat sugars, oil, and eggs, then mix in pumpkin. Fold in dry ingredients and chocolate chips.
2. **Bake:** Divide into muffin cups and bake at 375°F (190°C) for 18-22 minutes.

Lemon Poppy Seed Cake

Ingredients:

- 2 cups all-purpose flour
- 1 1/2 teaspoons baking powder
- 1/2 teaspoon baking soda
- 1/4 teaspoon salt
- 1/2 cup unsalted butter, softened
- 1 1/4 cups granulated sugar
- 2 large eggs
- 1 teaspoon vanilla extract
- 1/4 cup lemon juice
- 1/2 cup milk
- 2 tablespoons poppy seeds

Instructions:

1. **Mix batter:** Combine dry ingredients. Beat butter and sugar, add eggs, vanilla, and lemon juice. Alternate mixing in dry ingredients and milk. Stir in poppy seeds.
2. **Bake:** Pour into a greased bundt pan and bake at 350°F (175°C) for 40-45 minutes.

Double Chocolate Peppermint Cookies

Ingredients:

- 1 cup unsalted butter, softened
- 1 cup granulated sugar
- 1/2 cup brown sugar
- 2 large eggs
- 1 teaspoon vanilla extract
- 1/2 teaspoon peppermint extract
- 1 3/4 cups all-purpose flour
- 1/3 cup cocoa powder
- 1 teaspoon baking soda
- 1/2 teaspoon salt
- 1 cup chocolate chips
- 1/2 cup crushed peppermint candies

Instructions:

1. **Make dough:** Cream butter and sugars. Add eggs, extracts, and dry ingredients. Fold in chocolate chips and peppermint.
2. **Bake:** Drop spoonfuls onto a baking sheet and bake at 350°F (175°C) for 10-12 minutes.

Raspberry Almond Thumbprint Cookies

Ingredients:

- 1 cup unsalted butter, softened
- 2/3 cup granulated sugar
- 1/2 teaspoon almond extract
- 2 cups all-purpose flour
- 1/2 cup raspberry jam

Instructions:

1. **Make dough:** Beat butter, sugar, and almond extract. Mix in flour.
2. **Shape cookies:** Roll into balls, press centers with thumb, and fill with jam.
3. **Bake:** Bake at 350°F (175°C) for 12-15 minutes.

Sticky Buns with Caramel Sauce

Ingredients:

Dough:

- 3 1/4 cups all-purpose flour
- 1/4 cup granulated sugar
- 2 1/4 teaspoons active dry yeast
- 1/2 teaspoon salt
- 3/4 cup warm milk
- 1/4 cup unsalted butter, melted
- 2 large eggs

Filling:

- 1/4 cup unsalted butter, softened
- 1/2 cup brown sugar
- 1 tablespoon cinnamon

Caramel Sauce:

- 1 cup brown sugar
- 1/2 cup unsalted butter
- 1/4 cup heavy cream

Instructions:

1. **Prepare dough:** Combine dry ingredients, then mix in warm milk, butter, and eggs. Knead until smooth and let rise for 1-2 hours.
2. **Add filling:** Roll out dough, spread with butter, and sprinkle with sugar and cinnamon. Roll up and slice into rolls.
3. **Make caramel:** Melt butter and sugar in a saucepan, then stir in cream. Pour into a baking dish and place rolls on top.
4. **Bake:** Bake at 350°F (175°C) for 25-30 minutes.

Sweet Potato Pie

Ingredients:

- 1 1/2 cups mashed sweet potatoes
- 1 cup evaporated milk
- 3/4 cup granulated sugar
- 1/2 cup brown sugar
- 2 large eggs
- 1/4 cup melted butter
- 1 teaspoon cinnamon
- 1/2 teaspoon nutmeg
- 1 teaspoon vanilla extract
- 1 unbaked pie crust

Instructions:

1. **Prepare filling:** Blend sweet potatoes, sugars, eggs, butter, spices, and vanilla. Slowly mix in evaporated milk.
2. **Bake:** Pour filling into the pie crust and bake at 350°F (175°C) for 50-60 minutes until set.

Chocolate Crinkle Cookies

Ingredients:

- 1 cup granulated sugar
- 1/2 cup vegetable oil
- 2 large eggs
- 1 teaspoon vanilla extract
- 1 cup all-purpose flour
- 1/2 cup cocoa powder
- 1 teaspoon baking powder
- 1/4 teaspoon salt
- Powdered sugar (for coating)

Instructions:

1. **Make dough:** Mix sugar, oil, eggs, and vanilla. Add dry ingredients. Chill dough for 1 hour.
2. **Bake:** Roll dough into balls, coat in powdered sugar, and bake at 350°F (175°C) for 10-12 minutes.

Lemon Snowflakes

Ingredients:

- 1 box lemon cake mix
- 1/3 cup vegetable oil
- 2 large eggs
- Powdered sugar (for coating)

Instructions:

1. **Make dough:** Mix cake mix, oil, and eggs. Chill dough for 30 minutes.
2. **Bake:** Roll dough into balls, coat with powdered sugar, and bake at 350°F (175°C) for 10-12 minutes.

Orange Cranberry Loaf Cake

Ingredients:

- 1 3/4 cups all-purpose flour
- 1 teaspoon baking powder
- 1/2 teaspoon baking soda
- 1/4 teaspoon salt
- 1/2 cup unsalted butter, softened
- 1 cup granulated sugar
- 2 large eggs
- 1/3 cup orange juice
- Zest of 1 orange
- 1/2 cup milk
- 1 cup fresh or dried cranberries

Instructions:

1. **Mix batter:** Combine dry ingredients. Beat butter and sugar, add eggs, orange juice, zest, and milk. Fold in dry ingredients and cranberries.
2. **Bake:** Pour into a greased loaf pan and bake at 350°F (175°C) for 50-60 minutes.

Maple Walnut Fudge

Ingredients:

- 3 cups granulated sugar
- 3/4 cup unsalted butter
- 2/3 cup evaporated milk
- 1/2 cup maple syrup
- 1/2 teaspoon vanilla extract
- 1 1/2 cups chopped walnuts

Instructions:

1. **Cook fudge:** In a saucepan, combine sugar, butter, milk, and syrup. Boil until the mixture reaches the soft-ball stage (234°F/112°C).
2. **Finish fudge:** Remove from heat, add vanilla and walnuts, and pour into a greased pan. Let cool and cut into squares.

Pecan Praline Cookies

Ingredients:

- 1/2 cup unsalted butter, softened
- 1 cup brown sugar
- 1 large egg
- 1 teaspoon vanilla extract
- 1 1/4 cups all-purpose flour
- 1/2 teaspoon baking soda
- 1/4 teaspoon salt
- 1 cup chopped pecans

Instructions:

1. **Make dough:** Beat butter and sugar, add egg and vanilla, then mix in dry ingredients. Fold in pecans.
2. **Bake:** Drop spoonfuls of dough onto a baking sheet and bake at 350°F (175°C) for 10-12 minutes.

Cherry Chocolate Chunk Cookies

Ingredients:

- 1 cup unsalted butter, softened
- 3/4 cup brown sugar
- 3/4 cup granulated sugar
- 2 large eggs
- 1 teaspoon vanilla extract
- 2 1/4 cups all-purpose flour
- 1/2 teaspoon baking soda
- 1/4 teaspoon salt
- 1 cup dried cherries
- 1 cup chocolate chunks

Instructions:

1. **Mix dough:** Cream butter and sugars. Add eggs and vanilla, then mix in dry ingredients. Fold in cherries and chocolate chunks.
2. **Bake:** Drop spoonfuls of dough onto a baking sheet and bake at 350°F (175°C) for 10-12 minutes.

Hazelnut Linzer Cookies

Ingredients:

- 1 cup unsalted butter, softened
- 2/3 cup granulated sugar
- 1/2 teaspoon vanilla extract
- 2 large egg yolks
- 2 cups all-purpose flour
- 1/2 cup ground hazelnuts
- 1/2 cup raspberry or apricot jam
- Powdered sugar (for dusting)

Instructions:

1. **Make dough:** Beat butter and sugar, add vanilla and egg yolks, then mix in flour and hazelnuts. Chill dough for 30 minutes.
2. **Shape cookies:** Roll out dough, cut into shapes, and bake at 350°F (175°C) for 10-12 minutes.
3. **Assemble:** Spread jam on one cookie, top with another, and dust with powdered sugar.